PRAISE FOR ANOSH IRANI AND *BUFFOON*

"An epic tale of love and betrayal, triumph and loss, connection and abandonment—the human story." — *Globe and Mail*

"The play... begins with Felix as a hopeful child... and tracks his growing cynicism around life and love... An involving journey."
— *Toronto Star*

"*Buffoon* is a marvel of solo storytelling. A circus-noir mono-drama that traces a clown's tragicomic life of abandonment and perdition, this latest play from Vancouver novelist/drama-tist Anosh Irani possesses intrigue and poetic imagery... A paragon of tonal control and captivating solo storytelling."
— *NOW Magazine* (NNNN)

"Irani's acrobatic plotting invigorates the familiar cultural fig-ure of the melancholy clown... A dark tale for our dark times with some laughs along the way and a gleam of hope that the broken can be mended and the unforgivable forgiven."
— *Vancouver Sun*

"Irani's storytelling is a mix of fanciful wordplay... punctuated by poetic insights." — *Stir*

"*Buffoon* is full of powerful moments and rich metaphor."
— *Broadway World*

"Masterful... A quietly dense, complex story of yearning, love denied and love given, a story of a clown looking at acceptance. Anosh Irani is a wonderful playw

"Truly wonderful theatrical clowning…[Through] Irani's heart-wrenching storytelling…the story seeks out and often finds the comedy in the tragedy of Felix's life…These bursts of humour exemplify how the clown can find foolishness in even the saddest of experiences…Anosh Irani's story will leave you with a feeling of emotional whiplash in the best way possible."
— *My Entertainment World*

"*Buffoon*…traces the evolution of a clown—thematically and conceptually—and his discovery of his art…[Irani] synthesizes slapstick with tragedy in a final moment that…lands with a shattering effect." — Drew Rowsome, *My Gay Toronto*

"A profound, beautiful tragedy…Captivating, emotionally taxing, and downright great." — *Mooney on Theatre*

"Irani is an esteemed novelist-playwright, and, perhaps, because he has a foot in both literary camps, he is able to fashion such deep characterizations for both page and stage. Irani has poured all his considerable skill into crafting a compelling portrait of Felix the clown in words…The marvel of Irani's script is just how much humour, cynical though it may be, he has put into Felix's storytelling." — Paula Citron

BUFFOON

BUFFOON

ANOSH IRANI

ANANSI

Published in Canada in 2021 and the USA in 2021 by House of Anansi Press Inc.
www.houseofanansi.com

25 24 23 22 21   1 2 3 4 5

Library and Archives Canada Cataloguing in Publication

Title: Buffoon / Anosh Irani.
Names: Irani, Anosh, 1974– author.
Description: A play.
Identifiers: Canadiana (print) 20210218495 | Canadiana (ebook) 2021021855X | ISBN
9781487009830 (softcover) | ISBN 9781487009847 (EPUB)
Classification: LCC PS8617.R36 B84 2021 | DDC C812/.6—dc23

Cover design: Alysia Shewchuk
Cover image: HRH Anand Rajaram in *Buffoon*; Tarragon Theatre
Production, 2019. Photo by Cylla von Tiedemann
Text design: Laura Brady
Typesetting: Lucia Kim

House of Anansi Press respectfully acknowledges that the land on which we operate
is the Traditional Territory of many Nations, including the Anishinabeg, the Wendat,
and the Haudenosaunee. It is also the Treaty Lands of the Mississaugas of the Credit.

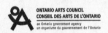

Canada Council   Conseil des Arts
for the Arts   du Canada

ONTARIO ARTS COUNCIL
CONSEIL DES ARTS DE L'ONTARIO
an Ontario government agency
un organisme du gouvernement de l'Ontario

With the participation of the Government of Canada
Avec la participation du gouvernement du Canada

We acknowledge for their financial support of our publishing program the Canada
Council for the Arts, the Ontario Arts Council, and the Government of Canada.

Printed and bound in Canada

MIX
Paper from
responsible sources
FSC® C103567
www.fsc.org

Buffoon premiered in Toronto in November 2019 at the Tarragon Theatre, Extraspace, under the artistic directorship of Richard Rose, with the following cast and creative team:

HRH Anand Rajaram as FELIX

Director: Richard Rose
Costume designer: Kathleen Johnston
Lighting designer: Jason Hand
Sound designer: Thomas Ryder Payne
Stage manager: Erika Morey
Assistant director: Jill Harper

*

Buffoon was given a public reading at the Arts Club Theatre Company's ReACT showcase in 2018. It was produced in Vancouver in October 2020 at the Arts Club Theatre Company, Granville Island Stage, under the artistic directorship of Ashlie Corcoran, with the following cast and creative team:

Kayvon Khoshkam and Andrew McNee, in alternating
performances, as FELIX

Director: Lois Anderson
Set designer: Amir Ofek
Costume designer: Christine Reimer
Lighting designer: Itai Erdal
Composer & sound designer: Joelysa Pankanea
Assistant director: Alexandra Lainfiesta
Stage managers: Caryn Fehr and Koh Lauren Quan
Apprentice stage managers: Heather Barr and Victoria Snashall
Dialect coach: Adam Henderson
Livestream director: Raugi Yu

HRH Anand Rajaram as Felix. Tarragon Theatre, Toronto.
Photograph by Cylla von Tiedemann.

(Above) Kayvon Khoshkam as Felix. Arts Club Theatre Company, Vancouver. (Below) Andrew McNee as Felix. *Set design by Amir Ofek; costume design by Christine Reimer; lighting design by Itai Erdal. Photograph by Moonrider Productions.*

BUFFOON

FELIX appears on stage, in a far corner. He is in his forties. Felix is a clown. But he is not a red-nosed clown. Felix is his own strange creation. His face is covered in white chalk. He is wearing a grey boilersuit.

A single chair on stage. The set looks like the visiting room in an old prison. It is. Nothing modern. The place seems far removed from the present. Bare walls. The only light on offer is a white tube light.

From his corner, Felix looks at the audience. He seems uneasy. Tender, shy, nervous. His nervousness is tangible. He isn't trying to make anyone laugh. He is a small, wounded creature.

FELIX   This is...

I don't know what to say.

The makeup... It's just chalk. Basic stuff.

Rudimentary. Like me.

I don't get too many visitors. So I thought I'd dress up for you.

He sits. He's not comfortable. He's trying to find a way to say something.

Look, I don't really know why you're here. I mean, I do, kind of. To be honest, I don't have much to say. I don't want to say anything, but now that you're here, I guess I do owe you some sort of…transmission.

Where do I begin?

He seems lost. Slowly, he looks at his right hand. It triggers something for him. Suddenly, his body contracts involuntarily like he's been seized by something.

FUTILE. FECKLESS. POINTLESS.

He puts his face in his hands. He quickly regains control.

Mark Twain said that the two most important days in your life are the day you were born and the day you find out why.

So let's start with the day I was born. Into the circus!

My mother, The Flying Olga, the darling of Leningrad…

He transforms into Olga, who speaks with a Russian accent and is always smoking a cigarette.

She hums "Sei Lieb Zu Mir."

The Flying Olga is sitting in her tent reading a beauty magazine, the kind where they promise you fresh skin but all that shows up on your face is sheer disappointment.

The Flying Olga's reading this, but she's not really *reading* reading. The Flying Olga's checking her own swollen face against theirs — all those derelict women, page after page of oblivious girls, completely unaware that this bomb's going to drop on their lives as well — and it must have caused her some distress because suddenly…

Her water breaks.

…and she's all alone in the tent, and the midwife…

OLGA   Mary the midwife!

            Felix, in an Irish accent: Who's not really a mid-
            wife but the head seamstress. She's probably
            tending to a costume emergency, which is more
            important than my birth — a tear in the tight
            rope walker's knickerbockers could result in a
            fatal plunge.

            So The Flying Olga has to get to the bathtub by
            herself, all the way over by the elephant pit...

OLGA   This is not contraction! This earthquake! Who
            I'm giving birth to — Genghis Khan? Frank!
            Frank! Get your sword. There is conqueror
            inside me. Holy shit, Frank! I think I just
            pooped. I pooped on your child's head. Does
            that tell you something?

            She finally gets there, but I'm halfway out
            between her legs, hanging upside down. Which
            makes total sense. My mother's a trapezist.

            As The Flying Olga hoists herself into the tub, I
            go back in.

OLGA   Come back out, you little shit!

FELIX   Hey, I could have hit my head, you know?

OLGA   That's what I was going for!

The Flying Olga positions herself to launch her little angel.

OLGA   We'll call it Lucifer, Frank!

And Smile fills the tub with water. Smile is the man who sells the tickets.

And my pops? The circus is on, my father is performing. He's flying through the air on the trapeze like Tarzan.

He swings like Tarzan and lets out an ape call.

My father makes a perfect landing. He is The Great Frank.

He stands like a strongman and starts bulging his biceps.

As I float to the surface of the tub and rise to the sound of applause. Five hundred people clapping just because I'm born.

I'm out! I'm a tiny piece of flesh and bone, and I'm out! Man, I'm out! I'm just a month old, but I've got all this joy, so I speak joy, and I've got all this song, so I sing song.

OLGA   Shut up, you freak!

	She just hears a baby who's colic.
OLGA	What you have done to me? What you have done?

Pops speaks with a Scottish accent.

POPS	But *you* said you wanted a child. *You* said you wanted one.
OLGA	I also say I want Mercedes. I want swimming pool. Where is Mercedes?
POPS	Take it easy now...
OLGA	Where is pool?
POPS	Relax, will you?
OLGA	Turn your sperm into Mercedes.
POPS	Yer bum's oot the windae. Yer nae making any sense.
OLGA	Where is pool?

Felix starts crying.

To shut me up, The Flying Olga puts talcum powder on my balls. To cool me down. And I just wanna thank her for all her efforts, you know? So I create giant puddles of love.

OLGA   He peed on me! Frank, he peed on me!

POPS   *There's* yer swimming pool!

That was when she went for him. She started chasing him around the tent, The Flying Olga after my pops like a torpedo.

The Flying Olga turns into a machine — she starts shedding fat like it's poison — and it's barely months since she's had me and she's back on the trapeze again. They leave me with Smile. Once he's sold his tickets, his job's done. Smile becomes my sitter. Smile takes to me, and I to him. And when I say my first word, he's there. And when I take my first step, he's there. And when I poop, he's outta there!

And Smile has a beard that's long, so damn long, but there's this wonderful smell, the smell of Smile, and I put my face in his beard and fall asleep, and the only time I wake up is when I'm under the Big Top again and Smile points to the sky, where I see The Flying Olga and Pops swinging from one branch to another, and I realize that The Flying Olga and Pops are not humans, they're birds, and if The Flying Olga's a bird, and if my pops is a bird, then I'm a bird too, and so I try to fly as well, I try to go toward them, I point to the sky, but Smile doesn't understand, so I start tugging at his beard, and he gets it, he lets go of me, and I hang...I just hang from his beard...That is how I started training to become a trapeze artist.

Felix conjures Smile with the simple stroke of his long beard. Smile speaks in a mellifluous English accent.

SMILE   You were born in water, and your parents live in the air. You need some earth. Flix, I want to show you something.

He takes me to his dwelling, and from underneath his bed he pulls out a large silver trunk. It's empty. Then he turns me around, makes me face the other way. I'm staring at this huge pile of books. He asks me what they are. One thing I don't like is a condescending adult.

FELIX   They're books, Smile.

SMILE   But you can't read them.

FELIX   Why not?

SMILE   Because you don't know how to read.

FELIX   Do *you*?

SMILE   Yes, Flix. That would be the whole point of this
             conversation.

FELIX   My name's Felix. Why do you keep calling me
             Flix?

SMILE   It's shorter. Now hurry up. There's no time to
             waste. Each book you read, you throw into the
             trunk. You have a trunk to fill. Start with this
             one: *Moby-Dick*. "Call me Ishmael." That's the
             first line. Remember that. Here.

             *When little Felix holds the book, he crumbles
             under its weight. Then he opens it and runs his
             fingers along the opening line.*

FELIX   Ish-ma-el.

             A small charge pulses through him as he reads.

             HARPOON.

             *A bigger charge. It's as though he's getting electri-
             fied by language. He says words out loud with the
             same sudden seize that overcame him at the
             beginning of the play.*

FELIX   MAMMIFEROUS. FLOODGATES. WONDER-
             WORLD.

SMILE   Calm down, Flix. Calm down.

But he just cannot help himself.

FELIX   CHEMICAL. INCREDIBLE.
IDIOSYNCRATIC. AFOREMENTIONED.
UNIVERSE.

He sees The Flying Olga. He points to her.

UNIVERSE. The AFOREMENTIONED
UNIVERSE.

OLGA   What you are talking about?

FELIX   Universe. It's a word.

OLGA   I know.

FELIX   It means the whole world. And more. You are
my universe.

OLGA   Right. *Beat.* Frank, we are doing the triple somersault.

POPS   No, we are not.

OLGA   We are. It's the only thing that will get us out of
this shitty circus. And that's that. *To Felix,* You.
Pass to me my cigarette and lighter.

*He fumbles with the cigarette and lighter. Olga's
getting impatient.*

Hurry up…

In his nervousness to get to her quickly, he trips and falls over.

Felix, how you fly in air if you can't even walk on ground?

FELIX   Sorry, I —

OLGA   Flick it on.

He does.

FELIX   COMBUSTION. COMBUSTIBLE.

She lights up. Inhales deeply.

OLGA   What the hell is wrong with you?

FELIX   Nothing, Mama.

OLGA   Mama? Who is that?

FELIX   Err…you?

OLGA   Me? No, no, munchkin. I'm nobody's mama.

She gracefully runs her hands down her body to signify her own magnificence.

I'm The Flying Olga.

FELIX   The Flying Olga...

OLGA   Right. A thing of beauty. A legend.

FELIX   But you're my —

OLGA   Call me Mama one more time, I tie you up to a
          tree and leave you behind. Frank, what's our
          next stop? We'll be traveling light. Now, now,
          don't cry. Okay, okay, come here. Come to
          Mama...

          But she gags when she says the word.

          Sorry, let's try that again. Come to Mama...

          Gags again.

          Please move. Give some air.

          *She exhales a cloud of smoke. Little Felix parts
          the cloud with his hands.*

          I start inhaling, in the hope that I might find
          something, some hint or clue that she loves me,
          some lingering smell of summer, of mama
          summer...But I just find smoke and more
          smoke, until—

Felix looks through the cloud of smoke, but instead of darkness, he sees something bright, something beautiful. He is hit by the thunderbolt of love. Full of longing, of seeing something truly beautiful for the very first time.

This vision, this APPARITION, this APOCALYPTIC beauty. I never noticed her before, but I'm a man now. I'm seven. She looks at me. She sees me.

He runs. He's panting like a madman.

FELIX   Smile! Smile! Smile!

SMILE   Why are you breathing so heavily? Do you have asthma?

FELIX   No, I saw this…I saw this…

SMILE   Dragon?

FELIX   No, I saw this…

SMILE   Wizard?

FELIX   No, I saw this…

SMILE   Orangutan!

FELIX   A *girl*, Smile. I saw a girl. She's golden, and she's in a stack of hay, and she's golden, and she's in a stack of hay...

SMILE   Oh dear.

FELIX   What?

SMILE   Oh my.

FELIX   What? What?

SMILE   Oh dear Allah.

FELIX   Smile!

SMILE   Tell me, Flix, how did you feel when you saw her?

FELIX   Like...puking?

SMILE   And how did you feel when she saw you?

FELIX   Like puking?

SMILE   And how do you feel right now?

Felix pukes.

I'm sorry to tell you this, Flix. But...I think you have Lovearia.

Felix is terrified.

FELIX   Lovearia? Oh my God!

Then he realizes he doesn't know what the word means.

What's that?

SMILE   It's like malaria. Only deadlier. You're in love, Flix. You've been bitten.

FELIX   *This* is what love feels like?

SMILE   This, and worse.

FELIX   Has this ever happened to you?

SMILE   A long, long time ago. But no matter. Life is good. Life is al-jabr.

FELIX   Al-what?

SMILE   Never mind. How old is she?

FELIX   Seven?

SMILE   Wait till she's eight.

FELIX   Are you insane? I'm sorry, I'm sorry. CATASTROPHIC. APOPLECTIC.

CATATONIC. SYPHILITIC.

SMILE   No, not syphilitic. The first three were fine. But
          relax, I'll give you something that will help. A
          sedative.

FELIX   A book?

SMILE   Robert Frost. "Miles to go before I sleep." Trust
          me, it won't take miles. You'll sleep there and
          then. Read it every night. Now wait till she's eight.

FELIX   What?

SMILE   Wait till she's eight.

          And I wait. Because it rhymes. In that waiting
          period, I find out everything there is. Her name
          is Aja.

          He says her name like it's magic.

          Aja… Aja… Aja…

          She is the adopted daughter of Mary the
          Seamstress. She's six months older than I am.
          I'm in love with an older woman. How erotic. I
          read everything there is to help me cope with
          my condition. Self-help books like *Romeo and
          Juliet*. That one was very helpful. The urge to be
          with someone can get so bad that you swallow

poison, and if you don't *time* the intake of poison correctly, you look like a nincompoop. When people speak of love, they don't tell you its true definition. It's not lilies and roses. It's kidneys and intestines. Waiting is hell. Maybe Pops can help me. It seems like he's always waiting. For Olga to love him. Who said that?

He looks for the culprit, though it is he who has said it.

What a horrible thing to say.

He runs to his tent.

FELIX   Pops, Pops.

POPS   *Ssh!* Quiet.

FELIX   Who's that man?

POPS   He's a journalist.

OLGA   We fly all day. That's what we do. We fly. Where I was born? How old I am? How does that matter? But if you must know, I was born in circus. Just outside of Moscow. I was child of circus parents, and my father was trapezist, and so was mother, it's like owning bakery, you know, you teach your kids how to bake, what can I say? Do I have children?

Little Felix's face lights up.

No. Don't have.

Little Felix is hurt.

Frank, who let this trainee into the room?

She snaps her fingers.

You. Cigarette. Lighter.

You mind if I smoke? When you're in the sky all day, a little smoke does you good, you know, it calms you down, it's like incense, some people light incense in their rooms, I light incense in my mouth, that's all. I'm twenty-three, and I'm in the best shape of my life.

FELIX   Twenty-three? You're not twenty —

OLGA   *Aside to Felix,* Do you know what cover story is? You cover your mouth.

Anyway, we are doing the triple somersault. Right, Frank?

Tell me, you have heard of this trapeze man, The Great Gagoonda? Oh yes…He wants to join our circus, but my husband, he is a bit, how

to say, possessive… to let me fly with another…
artist. Aren't you darling?

POPS   That will nae happen. And I'll tell you why. The
trapeze is about two things. It's about trust. And
love.

FELIX   Love?

POPS   When The Flying Olga does a somersault in the
air, there's no net below. If she falls, she breaks
her neck. She trusts I am the net that will catch
her. When we hold hands, it means *everything*.

FELIX   Pops, you're a genius.

I run to the stack of hay where Aja sleeps and
where she stares at the stars. Now I know what
love is. Love is about trust. She trusts I am the
net that will catch her. I will catch her, watch
her wiggle like a fish, and she is mine forever,
caught in my net… No, that's just… That's not
love at all… I need my pops to talk to me. He
put it so eloquently. Pops!

By the time I come back, the journalist's gone.

POPS   I said no.

OLGA   What happened to man I married? Where he is?

And the minute she says that, my pops starts to shrink. This hulk of a Frank, with tree trunks for legs and boulders for biceps, becomes smaller and shorter. All she has to do is pose a few questions and Pops just keeps getting smaller and smaller.

He becomes his father, shrinks and deflates, until he is down on his knees.

I had no idea questions could be so powerful. Will Aja have questions for *me*?

Each night, while everyone's asleep, I stand outside her tent.

This night, she appears. My future wife, my future everything, oh, what I would do for you...

I walk toward her carrying all that is gentle inside me, with the only thing I can truly offer...

He takes his tender heart out of his chest. It pulses in his palm.

Then he stops.

But...no...no...There's someone else with her, a *boy*...But maybe it's her brother, yes, oh, what

a relief, it's her brother…For a second there I
thought…Wow…This love thing is harsh…
But…

His heart starts beating ridiculously hard and fast.

…do brothers and sisters kiss on the lips?
Maybe it's a cultural thing. Maybe where she
comes from, they…Whoa, that's a whole lotta
tongue…That's the tentmaker's son!

*His heart pounds like mad and then falls to the
floor. He bends down. Picks it up. But it's all
squishy and messed up. The wreck that it is, it
slips through his fingers. He runs over to The
Flying Olga.*

FELIX   Mama…Mama…

*Olga raises one side of the eye mask a tad and
looks at her son with one eye.*

Ma…I mean, The Flying Olga…

OLGA   What is it?

FELIX   I…

He shows her his demolished heart.

FELIX   I hate her! I hate him! Is this what love does?

Olga sits up straight. She decides to give Felix an audience, a rare one. Felix lights a cigarette for her.

OLGA   Love is for puppy. You can love puppy forever. But human... just like cigarette smoke. My first cigarette, I cough, cough, cough. After some time, I get used to smoke. I don't cough anymore. Same with love. One day there is no hate left. That is end of love. You feel...nothing.

FELIX   But my heart —

OLGA   Do whatever buys you comfort, munchkin. Goodnight.

And as she sleeps, I look to the other side of the bed and it's empty. Pops is sleeping on the floor.

FELIX   Pops, Pops...

But when Pops opens his eyes, in them I recognize myself. He has the same haunted look that I have. And I just place my hand on his heart and put him back to sleep.

FELIX   Smile, Smile!

SMILE   What's wrong?

Felix shows Smile his squidgy heart.

SMILE   Oh…that's just…That's terrible. My condo-
         lences. The state it's in, pathetic, hideous…

FELIX   Smile!

SMILE   Okay, fine.

         *He uncorks a bottle of wine. Pours the burgundy
         liquid into a glass. Then he takes Felix's heart
         and drops it into the wine. He swirls it.*

FELIX   What's that?

SMILE   Medicine. Drink.

         Felix drinks. Hates the taste.

         Drink.

         *Felix drinks some more. Suddenly, the mixture
         does him some good. He drinks his heart and it
         settles back into place, starts swirling with vital-
         ity again.*

         Do you know who Li Po is? Of course you don't.
         Li Po was the greatest poet who ever lived.

FELIX   Listen, fuck poetry, okay?

         He drinks some more.

I'm not in the mood.

And some more. Drunk, he starts slurring.

Fuck all poetsh…

He keeps drinking. The slurring gets worse.

I'm solly, I'm solly. Pliss tell me about Lee Poah.

SMILE   He, like so many poets, found the moon beguiling. One night, after drinking a whole tumbler of wine, he went for a boat ride. He looked up at the moon and felt a great anguish that he was so far away from it, that even though he wrote about it, he would never really *know* it until he touched it. So, he decided he would stop looking at the moon once and for all. But then, as he looked down, he saw the moon again. He saw its reflection in the water. It was close. So close that he could touch it. And he reached into the water and tried to feel it, to know it, to embrace it.

FELIX   Good for him.

SMILE   He drowned. Do you see what I'm saying? If you become obsessed with the moon, you drown.

FELIX   I'm drowning, Smile. I'm drowning.

SMILE   I know that, you idiot. That's why I'm telling

you this story. You're AWOL.

FELIX   What's AWOL?

SMILE   Absent Without Love.

FELIX   Yes. Yes. Without her, I'm not even here.

SMILE   That is something the great Li Po would have said.

FELIX   Really?

SMILE   No.

Smile rolls up a monster joint.

Here.

FELIX   What's that?

SMILE   A baby elephant. That, my friend, is for AWOL.

Felix takes a major toke.

You're here, but you won't *know* you're here.

FELIX   Why do they call it a baby elephant?

The second he says that he gets super high. He raises his trunk and blows out a trumpet sound.

And this great peace comes over me, and I walk to the trapeze and I start swinging, and suddenly I am completely languid, a Li Po of the trapeze, and the circus lights become my moon...and I see this shark swim across the moon, *my* moon. Our circus has a new member: The Great Gagoonda!

He becomes The Great Gagoonda — embodies him, a giant.

He's bigger than Pops, bigger and meaner and taller. Fearless.

SMILE Just don't go near that man. There's something cold about him. If he holds a can of beer it will freeze.

And I see my Olga looking at him, and I do not like that look.

OLGA He'll be good for us. He'll make us famous. We can charge much more.

POPS No, I won't allow it.

OLGA I've already hired him, Frank.

POPS Then fire him!

OLGA I won't. I *will* do the triple somersault with The

Great Gagoonda. Just the name inspires confidence in me, Frank. Gagoonda! THE GREAT GAGOONDA! He's a beast from some remote island! A bird with muscles of iron! A god from another planet!

POPS   Sweetheart, his real name is Bob Edwin.

OLGA   What you refuse to do for me, he will.

And then she storms out of the tent. The Flying Olga climbs the rope, ascends to the heavens while Pops stays on the ground. The Great Gagoonda is already there, ready to catch her, ready to take his place.

FELIX   Pops, what do we do?

POPS   She won't listen.

FELIX   You have to do it. The triple somersault! Get up there! Go!

POPS   I can't. I don't have the courage. To lose her. To see her fall.

FELIX   It's okay, Pops. It's okay. You're The Great Frank! Where are you going? Pops?

My pops is disappearing.

	Smile, what's happening with my life?
SMILE	This *is* life, Flix. This is life.
FELIX	All war, no peace?
SMILE	You need to stop reading Tolstoy. He's fucking you up.
FELIX	The Flying Olga's with Gagoonda. The love of my life is with a *tentmaker's* son.
SMILE	Do you want to feel better?
FELIX	No more dope, Smile.
SMILE	No dope.
FELIX	And no more Li Po.
SMILE	And no more wine either, okay? You're an alcoholic.
FELIX	Then what? What can make me feel better?
SMILE	Chicken pox.
FELIX	Chicken pox?
SMILE	Your lady love has chicken pox.

FELIX   Shit. Poor thing. No, I mean screw her.

SMILE   You're dumb, Flix. She's contagious. She's
             scared. Bored. Alone. She is in a tent *alone*.

FELIX   So? Won't that dumb creep keep her company?

SMILE   He cannot. She's contagious. But *this* dumb
             creep can.

FELIX   Me? I don't want chicken pox!

SMILE   You had chicken pox when you were very little.
             You cannot get it twice.

FELIX   Oh.

             Then he understands what Smile is trying to tell
             him.

             Oh…

SMILE   Now go. Go, young man, and claim what is
             yours! What your looks and personality could
             not do, chicken pox will!

             I'm at the entrance to her tent.

             But he's super nervous. He breathes.

             Take it easy. Restraint. That's the order of the day.

He opens the tent. Enters.

Hi!

No restraint at all.

His eyeballs expand, become massive bugs, as though he has just seen the Kohinoor. He is a total nervous moron, dazzled.

I just love your boils.

I mean, even with those boils…

I should stop about the boils.

Sorry, I don't have a clue, what should I do? I didn't bring chocolates…I've heard that's a thing…I could drink poison. I've read guys do that for the women they love. Or I could slit my wrists. I can even slit my throat if you like. Or, better still, how about I cut my entire head off and lay it by your feet? As a mark of respect, of course. I should have brought flowers. But flowers wilt.

He embodies Aja as she twirls her curls with her fingers.

AJA   And a skull is forever?

FELIX   Huh?

            Then he gets that she gets it. They have a connection.

AJA   My name's Aja. But you already knew that.

FELIX   But to hear it from you...Oh my God, it's like...

            He indicates that his brain is exploding.

            ...can you say your name again?

AJA   Aja?

FELIX   Aja...Aja...Aja...

AJA   You do know what my name means, right?

FELIX   Of course, of course. Actually, I don't.

AJA   Come hither.

FELIX   Sure...

AJA   No, that's what my name means in India. Come hither.

FELIX   Wowza.

He starts walking toward her in a trance as his thesaurus unleashes:

FELIX   PERSPICACIOUS. SAGACIOUS. AUDACIOUS. BODACIOUS.

AJA   Don't come too close.

FELIX   It's okay…

AJA   I have chicken pox.

FELIX   I don't care.

AJA   Don't come any closer! Have you ever had chicken pox before?

FELIX   No, never. Never. I have never ever had chicken pox before. Ever.

AJA   Then you could get it.

FELIX   Who cares? If I do, I do. How old are you?

AJA   Twelve.

FELIX   So am I. I'm twelve. Where's your…um… friend? The…tentmaker's son.

AJA   He can't come near me. He's never had chicken pox.

FELIX   That's a bit selfish, isn't it? Or maybe he's just
             plain chicken.

AJA   It's nice of you to come.

FELIX   It's the least I can do...even though you deci-
             mated my heart.

AJA   Whenever I look at you, you're always looking
             down. I've been trying to talk to you since I was
             five.

FELIX   I was waiting for the right time.

AJA   And the time is now? When I'm sick?

FELIX   I...

AJA   I'm just teasing you.

FELIX   Is it okay with you if I shake your hand?

AJA   You want to shake my hand?

FELIX   Yes. I'm sorry...It's okay if you don't want to.
             It's just that I'm a huge hand-shaker.

AJA   But I have the pox.

FELIX   I don't care.

AJA   I have a boyfriend.

He moves toward her. He channels Pops.

FELIX   But when *I* hold your hand…

He holds her hand.

…it means *everything*.

She gets it. I've embraced her pustules, therefore
every single part of her. Thanks, Pops. We hold
hands and walk across the circus grounds, as
small white tents float in the breeze. Smiles all
around from the lion tamer, the tightrope
walker, the jugglers, making our union offi-
cial…and as I pass the tentmaker's son, I do a
little dance and twirl Aja around.

Across the elephant pit we go, until we finally
reach the other end of the circus. "This is the
tub in which I was born. One day, this tub will
be yours." Women just love a man with prop-
erty. We lie in the tub.

He sits next to her, nervous. Kind of prepares
himself to kiss her. But by the time he faces her…

She's tired, she closes her eyes. It's okay, we have
the rest of our lives. There's a lantern near the
tub. I use it to light a cigarette. Nothing says

you're mine like a cigarette.

He blows heart-shaped smoke rings.

*Lights change. We are back in the prison again.
Stark white light, bare walls.*

Anyway, that's how we...got together. It was...
maybe...the moment of my life...But something wonderful is always followed by
something...else.

Lights change. He is back in the tub.

I stare at the stars. It's so quiet. Everyone has
gone to sleep.

I smell something. Something's burning. It's not
my cigarette.

FELIX   Hey! Hey! Aja, the Big Top's on fire!

AJA   What?

FELIX   You stay here!

There's a figure running in the dark.

Hey, you!

I pounce on him.

Pops! Pops?

The shame is dripping from his face.

POPS   You did not see me. I was nae here.

By then, everyone's awake. Mary the Seamstress,
the lion tamer, the elephant trainer, the ring-
master, the juggler — they all turn into firemen.

They quell the fire.

They ask me if I saw something. I look for my
father. He's nowhere to be seen. I tell them the
guy who did it ran into the woods. Aja just
looks at me.

That night, I curl up right next to Pops and we
just breathe together, father and son. Tomorrow,
The Flying Olga was supposed to be doing the
triple somersault. With Gagoonda.

But what about the day after tomorrow, Pops?
Will you light a fire every night?

The next morning, Pops is a new man.

POPS   They have days to rebuild the tent.

OLGA   Frank, you're not strong enough. Not quick
enough. Not anymore.

POPS   You will practice the triple somersault with me. That's an order.

And off they go. He is tiny no more. He is a beast. The Great Gagoonda is nowhere to be seen. My pops is high up there, like Tarzan, and I hear apes from some distant jungle...

He beats his chest and lets out ape sounds.

...their open mouths and jagged teeth eating the jungle air. And I stand below, in awe of this majesty, of these two beings who are my parents, The Great Frank and The Flying Olga... And the Tarzan of the Trapeze starts swinging, the wind is carrying him, to and fro, to and fro, to and...My pops is on the ground...He's huge...a huge, huge mess. The Flying Olga...

The Flying Olga freezes. She lets out a silent scream.

That day everyone hovers at the entrance to our tent. Gagoonda shows up. Aja holds me. I see him whisper something to The Flying Olga. Maybe he feels bad about Pops. Or maybe he smells the blood in the water.

I push Aja away. For the first time, I push her away from me.

OLGA   Here, Frank, eat. You have to eat, Frank.

            But Pops refuses to eat. The Flying Olga gives up
            and passes the bowl to Felix.

            The Flying Olga never gets her Mercedes.
            Instead, Frank gets a wheelchair.

OLGA   Please. You have to eat.

            Maybe Pops couldn't bear the humiliation of
            having The Flying Olga clean him.

FELIX   Here, Pops, eat. You have to eat. Please.

            But he'd just sit there, all by himself...wet...
            smelling his own future.

            Before every show, he'd foam at the mouth. It
            was quite something, a little spit cloud that he
            wanted us to decipher.

            What are you trying to say, Pops?

            One night I am awakened by a strange music.
            The Flying Olga is drunk.

            She hums "Sei Lieb Zu Mir."

            My father sneezes, but even that is beautiful.

The Flying Olga leans in, whispers something to him. "Frank, I..."

I cannot hear the rest.

The next day is a big day for The Flying Olga. It is the day she finally performs the triple somersault with The Great Gagoonda. Posters have been made. Smile runs out of tickets. But he isn't happy. He knows something. No one says anything, but there is an unspoken knowledge in the air, the way animals know a storm is coming.

I go to my tent to wish The Flying Olga luck. But she isn't there. The show begins. The Great Gagoonda and The Flying Olga are up in the air, flying together... They make it look so easy... It's as if when they hold hands, it means *everything*.

They wow the audience, but with each turn, I shrink, with each swing, I shrink, with each flip, I shrink, and in a final flourish, The Great Gagoonda whisks my mother away — up into the sky they go, hand in hand, they migrate like a pair of geese, and leave this gosling behind.

He reaches for his mother with love and longing. But she's gone.

When I come back to the tent, I find a note. It's on my bed and it's from my Olga.

"Dear Felix…"

That's all the note says. The Flying Olga has left it blank. What does it mean? Was she trying to tell me that I could complete the letter, write whatever I wanted because it was my story? *Write whatever buys you comfort, munchkin.*

I choose to leave it blank. But I add one line at the end. "From your ever-loving Olga." To add anything more would be an act of treason. This was an act of hope.

It's okay, I get it… She fell in love. She chose love. One love over another kind of love. She knew I'd be fine. After all, how long can you mother someone?

SMILE   Flix, it's okay, it's okay…

FELIX   I know. I'm fine. I'm fine.

SMILE   You're not fine. And neither is your mother.

FELIX   What do you mean?

SMILE   She always wanted to be in the movies. Like Marlene Dietrich. In her mind, she's a movie star.

FELIX   Don't movie stars have children?

SMILE   Of course they do. But not while they're stuck in
           the circus. You see what I'm saying? She'll never
           be able to love you until she finds what she's
           looking for.

FELIX   And what if she doesn't?

SMILE   You can't wait for her to love you, Flix.

FELIX   But she's my mother.

SMILE   She's a human being. Just like you. Like me.

           Mothers. What is it about them? What makes it
           so hard for us to accept that they might not love
           us? That they may have never wanted us in the
           first place? The womb is a sticky place. Warm
           and cozy, you spend the rest of your life trying
           to find a room just like it. Wombs are tombs. It
           rhymes.

           And Pops keeps getting smaller. Smaller and
           lighter.

           *He lifts the wheelchair with one hand, with Pops
           in it, as though he is doing a shoulder press.*

FELIX   Hey, Pops, look at this. I can lift your wheelchair
           with one hand. Come on, Pops, you gotta eat.

*Then he brings the same hand down and presents
Pops like a server would a tray.*

I'll feed you to the lions, Pops. I'm warning you.
Hey, Pops, I guess they don't like spaghetti.
Because that's what you are. A noodle!

Get up, man! Fight back! Say something!

I know what you did, Pops. You fell on purpose,
didn't you?

*Suddenly Pops starts making crackling sounds as
though he is trying to say something.*

FELIX   What is it, Pops?

Pops, you're talking! I'm here, Pops. Talk to me,
I'm here.

There's this cloud of spit at the edge of his lips,
so big, so beautiful.

POPS   She loves the sea...even though...it foams.

Those are his last words to me.

One night, I wake up to the sound of him chok-
ing. I can hear him but I can't see him. Pops?
He's not in his wheelchair. I go outside and spot
him: this cloud of foam, like a soap bubble, it

goes up in the air, and I understand what he's trying to do…He's going after The Flying Olga the only way he knows how. "I love you, Pops." I see the last of him disappear.

On the bright side, there's nothing left for me to bury. Imagine trying to bury a soap bubble. Can't have an open casket, that's for sure.

It was hard for me to get rid of his wheelchair. I'd sit in it, alone in my tent, and blow bubbles. I would whisper messages to each bubble, you know?

AJA   You're blowing soap bubbles all day, Felix. You've been sitting in that chair for a month, blowing bubbles.

FELIX   These aren't bubbles. That's Pops. I'm blowing my father. Sorry, that sounded weird.

There was this abandoned ski slope close to the circus. I take the wheelchair there and sit in it, at the top. Pops was a man of grace and movement, and he needed to go with the grace and speed he deserved.

He sits in the wheelchair and rolls downhill.

"Hey Pops, it's all downhill from here!"

The wheelchair hits a bump and I crash straight into a tree.

He holds his broken leg.

The pain shoots through me like a snakebite.

A passerby looks at me and laughs. "What a buffoon."

What a buffoon.

A stranger shows me who I am.

A buffoon. An idiot. A clown. In the circus, he is the ANTITHESIS NEMESIS of the acrobat. I can never be a trapezist because I am the enemy.

Twain was right: The two most important days in your life are the day you were born and the day you find out why.

I *am* a buffoon.

I'm thirteen years old and I'm still terrified of kissing Aja.

He limps toward Aja.

Aja, you know, from the time I met you...Listen,

I'm done talking. Why talk?

Why not make love? Make love to me, Aja.
We're both thirteen. It's an unlucky number,
but we might get lucky.

AJA   Just so we're clear, this will be *your* first kiss, not
          mine.

FELIX   Sure, sure, whatever ... Let's just kiss.

          He sits down, nervous, excited.

          *He puckers his lips. Nervous, excited. Clasps his
          hands.*

          Moves in to kiss her. But gets a hiccup.

          *Embarrassed, he clears his throat. Tries again.
          Another hiccup. Oh dear.*

          *Aja laughs. Felix notices that she has laughed.
          He gets a bit emboldened by her laugh.*

          *Now, he takes out a mouth spray, shakes it, and
          then sprays it into ... his eye. What an idiot. Then
          he tries again, sprays his other eye. Aja laughs.*

          *He finally gets it right. He sprays it in his mouth
          but hates the taste. So he uses his hand to wipe
          the taste away.*

In doing so, he suddenly realizes that he loves the taste of his own hand. With his other hand, he covers his face, preventing Aja from seeing him, and continues kissing his hand. The lazzo of the first kiss is born.

AJA   You're so weird.

FELIX   But you laughed.

AJA   I'm still waiting for you to kiss me.

FELIX   But you're laughing.

           And the next thing I know, I'm kissing myself in front of five hundred people. My first kiss becomes my first act.

           Now he is performing in front of a circus audience.

           He continues with the lazzo of the hand. His hand is now a love interest. With his other hand, he holds a small box. Pops it open to reveal a wedding ring. He proposes. His bride is ecstatic.

           He makes his hand (bride) wear the ring. Wedding music plays as they walk down the aisle. He kisses her. Applause from the circus audience.

           He takes a bow after his performance.

SMILE   Come on, Flix. Let's go.

FELIX   Go? Where?

SMILE   It's your birthday today, moron.

FELIX   But I've never celebrated my birthday before.
          Really?

SMILE   No. Where is that girlfriend of yours?

FELIX   I don't know…

SMILE   She's sixteen now, Flix. Keep an eye on her. At
          sixteen, the brains short-circuit. They fizz and
          pop like soda.

FELIX   *I'm* sixteen, too.

SMILE   Exactly. But she's good looking. You, on the
          other hand…

FELIX   Deeply noted.

SMILE   Yalla.

FELIX   What?

SMILE   Let's go.

          The three of them walk. Smile, Aja, and Felix.

We're in a small town our circus travels to once every few months. But I've never ventured outside before. I see all these telephone poles. So many telephone poles.

AJA   Those are *people*, Felix.

FELIX   Oh.

We arrive at this mansion. There's a small plastic puddle and there are these little creatures, these horrendous —

AJA   They're children, Felix.

FELIX   They're so … disgusting.

They're so scary; they have these powerful lungs and can scream at will, can yell for anything and it just magically appears, like "I want juice," and it fucking appears. "I want a biscuit," and it fucking appears. "I wanna pee," and the water turns yellow. I walk around the pool, afraid that they might spot me, ask *me* for something. But Aja, she moves *toward* them, the guts this woman has, and I keep reminding her about those safaris in Kenya where you stay *in* the jeep, you know, you do not get *off* the jeep, but she doesn't care, she just moves toward them, and they respond to her so … so *lovingly*, they crawl all over her like lice …

I've seen kids all my life in the circus. You can spot them in the audience in a second. They have this halo, this circle of light around them that's actually meant to be a warning, but instead people gravitate *toward* them. Buy them ice cream. Kids don't really like ice cream. They like licking something cold, the way the devil does, sitting in hell, licking dead bodies.

Lights change. He is back in prison. He realizes he has said something hurtful.

I'm sorry, this is too much, this is... I'm sorry, I shouldn't be saying this to you... I won't talk about kids anymore. Let's... talk about the circus instead. Yes, the circus...

Lights change. He goes back to his crazed monologue.

Who the hell do you think they're for? Children! Animals parading around wearing clothes when they could be naked in the wild, copulating in peace. Clowns tumbling and falling so that little William, fuck him, can have a giggle. The circus is no laughing matter! People fall, they get crippled!

He looks at the sky.

Hey, Pops! Did little William buy you a wheel-chair?

No. Once the show's over, they leave their candy wrappers and paper napkins and go home like it was some...picnic. Picnics! Don't get me started on picnics. One of mankind's most nau-seating creations. And children are responsible. You wake up early, you make sandwiches, lem-onade, Band-Aid, whatever; you drive for miles with little William and Greta raising hell in the back seat, all of you in a bad mood, until you reach...Oh...look at that...a *pond*. All those horrible arguments, the unrequited love, the mortgage, the desire, actually, to be with some-one else, *anyone* else — it's all worth it because in the end, husband, wife, little William and Greta are by a *pond*. And while you stare at the pond, and little Willie and Greta play, you sing nursery rhymes and hope that one of them takes a dip in the pond when you're not looking.

And then you go home with one child instead of two, and my oh my, does the car feel lighter. But — little Willie misses Greta. He misses pull-ing her hair and setting her dress on fire. So you decide, "Ah, a pet! That's what I'll get!" A par-rot, a rooster, a cat, a hamster? No, how about that most noble of creatures: A dog! A Rottweiler. An untrained one...because unlike circus folk we want our animals to be who they are. And then you watch Little William play with the Rottweiler, and you go, "Look at that, our William's not afraid of dogs. Isn't that great?" But little William's not afraid of anything. He's a serial killer.

But by then William's captured you with his overall charisma. You're obsessed with him. Have you noticed how parents can't talk about anything else? Oh, my child walked today, my child talked today, *aww*, he pooed today, my baby, did you just poo...did you just do a big poo-poo? Oh, you vomited, you *wahmetead*. And don't get me started about parents who have twins. Oh, look at us, we're twice as good. No, you're twice as stupid.

These marvellous adults with lives and skills and intelligence become blabbering wrecks, terrified that their child won't sleep. Sleep: that's a big one for parents. Imagine being scared that someone won't sleep. What if I said to you, "Hey, I won't sleep tonight." Well, fuck you, don't sleep.

The act of bringing a child into this world: stupidity. The child agreeing to enter:

He indicates himself.

buffoonery.

Aja comes toward me, covered in child slime.

BUBONIC. TECTONIC. BUFFONIC.

AJA   I'd love to have a house with a pool someday...
           filled with kids.

FELIX   ABOMINATION. DETESTATION.

AJA   Felix, for once, can we just...*not* be weird?

FELIX   FRANKENSTEIN NATION.

AJA   Felix, relax. I don't want any of those things,
           okay? I was just...imagining.

FELIX   Then imagine better things! Imagine all those
           beautiful children in that cute little pool, drown-
           ing. All of them, all at once, but then...one
           survives, by stepping all over the others...He
           crawls over the side, and falls, and grows up...to
           become...a writer...and he thanks them all in
           his autobiography...which is called... *Yay: It
           could have been me...but it wasn't...It was them.*

AJA   Smile! Get him outta here!

           Aja goes back to the pool.

FELIX   I need a drink. I need ten drinks. I need a brew-
           ery. I need —

SMILE   You need a tight slap. That's what you need.

               I enter the house with Smile.

               There's a man Smile's age, and his wife, and they
               hug him. And the man hands Smile a letter...

               The letter makes Smile serious.

FELIX   What's wrong, Smile?

               Smile hands Felix the letter. Felix takes the letter,
               worried. But —

               What the hell? What language is this?

SMILE   Pashto.

FELIX   I can't read Pashto. How do *you* know Pashto?

SMILE   Because of where I'm from.

FELIX   They speak Pashto in England?

SMILE   Afghanistan.

FELIX   Afghanistan? But you're from England.

SMILE   Not at all. Just stayed there for a bit. Used the
               accent to sound more cultured, less threatening.
               Even though they conquered half the world,

their accent is quite delightful. People found it
very —

FELIX   Smile, I'm not people!

SMILE   Oh. My name isn't Smile, either.

FELIX   WHAT?

SMILE   It's Ismail.

FELIX   ISMAIL?

SMILE   Flix, Felix. Smile, Ismail. Same thing. Just
             shorter. The people here didn't get my name.
             People kept calling me "Smile." So I smiled
             back.

FELIX   I'm not *people*! Will you stop calling me *people*?
             Why didn't you tell me?

SMILE   I did. *Moby-Dick*. "Call me Ishmael." It's the
             first line you ever read.

FELIX   This is fucked up.

SMILE   No. What's fucked up is this. This letter…It's
             from my village. My neighbour. It's about my
             family. When I was a young man, I worked with
             my father on my land. We had a lot of land. It
             was very fertile land. We grew poppy. The thing

is, everyone wanted poppy. And there was this warlord who wanted it more than anyone else. So, he gave me a choice. If I did not leave the country, go far away, he would kill my entire family and take my land. If I left, he would spare my family and take my land. Now you will ask, "Why didn't he kill you, your family, and take your land?" These people like to think they have honour. It is the way men were back then in Afghanistan. Now they're all gone.

FELIX   What do you mean? Who's gone?

SMILE   Mother, father, sisters … all gone. Dead.

FELIX   I'm sorry. I'm sorry, who the hell *are* you?

SMILE   I'm … me. A man with a past. That's all.

FELIX   That's *all*? What do you mean that's all? That's a lot! Is there anything else?

SMILE   No. Well, there is one thing.

FELIX   You have a wife? A son? Another family waiting for you somewhere?

SMILE   It's about the tickets.

FELIX   Tickets? What tickets?

SMILE   The tickets I've been selling.

FELIX   Who gives a hoot in hell about tickets?

SMILE   That's not the only thing I've been selling. Like I
             said, Afghanistan is known for its poppy.

FELIX   So?

SMILE   I've been using the circus to sell *dope*, Flix. This
             house, this man, he's my supplier.

FELIX   You're a drug dealer?

SMILE   That's a bit harsh. Let's just —

FELIX   You're a DRUG DEALER?

SMILE   Let's just … I supply AWOL.

FELIX   You lied to me. Your whole life … my whole
             life … I trusted you, Smile. Why'd you lie to me?

SMILE   Because I couldn't let you see that I was broken.
             The last thing you needed was one more adult
             who was broken.

FELIX   Don't say that. You're not broken.

SMILE   When you can no longer be who you are, you're
             broken. They couldn't even get my name right,

Flix! Ismail, Ismail, Ismail! I kept saying it
again and again! And they kept going, Smile?
Smile? Smile? And one day, I realized they were
telling me to put *on* a smile, put a smile on
everything because they didn't *care* where I was
from or what I had been through. I just had to
smile and *behave* myself and fit in because this
land was theirs, not mine, and never would be!
Do you understand what that's like?

*For the first time, Smile has vented his anger and
frustration.*

I just…want to go home.

FELIX   So do I. Get me out of here. Please.

SMILE   No, I mean home. Now that my family's gone, I
            can finally go back home.

FELIX   But…but…why do you want to go home if
            there's no one?

SMILE   To die…

FELIX   Why not die here? At least here you'll have
            someone to look after you when you're old. I'll
            always look after you, Smile. Even if you lose
            complete control of your bowels. I'll clean your
            arse until you're dead, I promise. Please stay.

SMILE   And do what?

FELIX   Anything. Stare at the moon.

SMILE   It's not my moon, Flix. It's not my moon.

FELIX   But *I'm* here.

SMILE   No, Flix...

Smiles takes Felix's hand and places it on his heart.

...You're *here*. You'll always be.

Felix recoils.

FELIX   Don't touch me! You're just like them! You're just like my pops and Olga!

And I realize that there's this umbilical cord that connects me to the only true parent I've ever had, and suddenly this kind, loving drug dealer starts rising in the air, like a balloon, and the cord gets elongated...

SMILE   I'm sorry, Flix. I'm so sorry...

FELIX   Fuck you, Smile.

I take a pair of scissors...

He cuts the cord as Smile flies away.

Fuck you. I mean, I love you. Fuck you. I love you. Go stare at your moon!

He is devastated. On his knees as he watches Smile sail away. He is in pain, barely able to utter the words.

Fuck you... I love you... Fuck you...

What will I do without you, Smile? What will I do without you?

SMILE   No matter. Life is good. Life is al-jabr, Flix. All life is al-jabr!

FELIX   What the hell does that mean? Tell me what it means!

SMILE   It means...

But Smile is too far away now.

FELIX   What? What does it mean?

And *Ismail* sails off to Afghanistan. And perhaps he gets to touch his moon on the way.

Felix catches something that Smile drops from the sky.

Smile's left something for me. One more blank
letter? One more stupid story that I have to
make my own?

AJA   Look, it's a map. It's a map of our circus.

FELIX   Why would he give us a map of the circus?

AJA   Hey, there's an X there. He wants us to find that
             spot.

             And off we go. To a tree in a corner of the
             ground. An old tree. I look around it, but I find
             nothing. By then, Aja is already high up.

AJA   There's something on that branch.

FELIX   It looks like a book.

             "Dear Flix, screw Chekhov and all the Russians.
             This writer made way more money."

             He reads the title:

             Memoirs of a Woman of Pleasure.

             Inside the book, hundreds of dollars between
             every page.

             "My royalties from 'selling tickets.' *Ha ha ha*.
             Inside my trunk, you'll find a huge ball of

Afghan dope. Your pension."

"Meanwhile, here's a baby elephant. Enjoy. And don't forget: All life is al-jabr."

FELIX   Here we go again with that al-jabr shit.

AJA   Algebra.

FELIX   What?

AJA   Al-jabr. That's the Arabic word for algebra.

FELIX   How do you know?

AJA   Smile told me.

FELIX   He told *you*? I mean, what the hell? He told *you*? What am I supposed to do with algebra? Realize that my life equals nothing? What kind of fucked up wisdom is that?

AJA   I think you need some of that Afghan poppy.

The two of them smoke. Felix raises his elephant's trunk, lets out a trumpet sound, and gets high.

FELIX   There's me. There's you. There's the moon. It's like Li Po himself is talking to me.

AJA   What's he saying?

FELIX	"Kiss her, Felix. Kiss her well, for a change."
AJA	He's a wise man.

He holds her chin as though he is about to plant the kiss of the century.

FELIX	To hell with wisdom. Here I come.

He kisses her.

Why are your lips so rough?

AJA	That's the tree trunk, Felix.

FELIX	Fuck. I'm useless.

AJA	Yes, my love. That much is true. From now on, I'm in charge. This is how you kiss.

She holds him. Gives him the kiss of the century.

Since she leads the way, it's more than a kiss. It's the entire continent…of Heaven.

I taste every part of her body, realize her strength, understand that even though she is an orphan, she has no sense of bitterness toward the world; she demands no vengeance, takes each day as it comes, teaches me to do the same, pre-pares meals that are simple and truthful, makes

me inhale steam with eucalyptus when my nose
is blocked, rubs my back when I cry for Smile
and makes me smile for him instead. From sixteen to twenty-one, I remain in that state of bliss.
Sometimes she sleeps alone in the hay, near the
bathtub, and when she wakes up and leaves at
night, I sleep in the same spot, the cavity of
warmth that she has carved, in the hope that I
might find some forgiveness toward this world,
which is her secret... If I could just learn to for-
give... that's the clown I would aspire to be.

One night, after a show, Aja comes to me.

He's removing his clown costume.

AJA   Felix?

FELIX   Pumpkin?

AJA   I was thinking...

FELIX   Yes?

AJA   There's something I wanted to...talk to you
          about...

FELIX   Sure, what is it?

AJA   It's...I...I just...Just stay calm...okay...

FELIX   It's the tentmaker's son, isn't it? You're attracted
         to him again after all these years. To his
         tent-making abilities. I mean, I will admit he
         can be endearing at times.

AJA   Felix, everything isn't a joke.

FELIX   Of course it is. If it isn't a joke, then it's life. And
         I don't do life.

AJA   What if...you had to?

FELIX   I don't have to do anything. I could just skip all
         day I if wanted to. I suggest you do the same.

         He starts skipping.

AJA   I need you to listen...

FELIX   And I need you to skip.

         He continues doing a ridiculous skip and dance.

         A long pause from Aja.

         *Then, she slowly puts her thumb into her mouth
         and blows on it. With her other hand, she forms
         a curve around her belly, as though she has just
         inflated a small balloon. The action is very gentle
         and loving.*

Felix sees what she is doing. He imitates her actions. Thumb, belly bloat. Then he presses his belly down to flatulate.

Once again, Aja bloats her belly by blowing on her thumb.

Once again, Felix does the same. But he does not release the flatulence this time. Instead, he puts on a helmet and a pair of goggles. Then he counts down with his fingers: 5, 4, 3, 2, 1. He puts a lighter under his bum and off he goes into the air like a rocket.

He greets birds along the way. Then he passes the moon. He is soon approaching the sun. But he is unstoppable. He is going straight into the sun. Aaargh! He explodes.

Then Felix suddenly breaks out of the act:

FELIX   My act is strong as it is. I don't see where this would fit in.

AJA   It's not an act.

FELIX   It's an act. It has to be.

She moves toward him. But not like a clown. Like a woman.

Don't do this.

AJA   Felix...please...

FELIX   Those things...You know how I feel.

AJA   They're not things.

FELIX   Can't you see what they did to me? My Olga and
           Pops?

AJA   But we'll be different. We'll be the opposite of
           what they were.

FELIX   I can't. I'm sorry. Maybe...Maybe a few years
           from now.

AJA   We don't have years. We have months.

           *She is soft and there is a glow about her, a
           strength, a confidence. She slowly takes his hand,
           holds it with all the love she has.*

           Because when I hold your hand...it means
           everything.

FELIX   How could you do this to me? I trusted you.

AJA   This child will know who its parents are. I never
           did. This child will. I want it to be a girl. I want
           her name to be Emma. Can we call her Emma?

Sometimes at night I used to call for my mama, and no one would come, so Emma sounds like mama, and when I call her name, someone will finally come.

She addresses her child.

We both love you a lot, you know. I never had a mama or a papa. So I have no idea what I'm doing. But we'll figure it out, okay? Just talk to me. Whatever it is, just talk to me. Hey, stop that. That's my umbilical cord. Felix, she's doing the trapeze! Felix, say something...Emma, I think it's time for you to chat with your papa. He says he's shy, but he's just high maintenance. Go on, Felix. Stop looking at my belly like that. She's in there. What do you think that is, last night's sandwich?

He slowly reaches out, touches her belly. He feels her pulsing heart.

FUTILE. FECKLESS. POINTLESS.

Lights change. He is in prison again.

Felix now speaks to the one person to whom he has been telling this story. His daughter: Emma.

When he speaks from this point on, it's simple and truthful. He can no longer hide behind

performance, poetry, or humour. There is no
audience anymore, just a father talking to his
daughter during a prison visit.

Emma, I...

Look, what do you want me to say?

I didn't want any of this...I started drinking...
much more...It got ugly...I was drinking one
night, and she was sleeping in the hay with
you...near the tub...and there was this lantern...you know...and I saw your face, you
were so soft...only a few months old...

...and instead of feeling love for you, I...I just
hated you...and it made me sick that I felt that
way...and...

...I picked you up to tell you how sorry I was
for feeling that way...and then you looked at
me...Why did you have to open your eyes? You
looked at me and I started crying...I promised
you I'd stop drinking...so I held you tight
against my chest and emptied the bottle on the
hay...as a promise...and then you cried, and
your mother woke up...and...she asked me to
hand you over as though I was some kind of...

But just as I was about to hand you over, she
leaned in toward me and whispered something

in my ear: "Felix, I…" I couldn't hear the rest…
It just reminded me of my Olga and how she
whispered something in my father's ear just
before she flew away…and I wouldn't let her do
that to me, so I refused to hand you over, that's
all…It was just a push…I just pushed her away,
nothing special, it was just a push…

…and the lantern must have fallen…and the
hay caught…and I almost dropped you, out of
fear…By then the flames…I thought your
mother went the other way…

…but she must have hit her head on the tub…
It's just one of those things…I mean, I *am* a
buffoon, after all…That's what I told the cops…
and I didn't mind going to jail because it would
keep me away from you; you'd be safe…

You look so much like her…

The only thing my Olga cared about was the
applause. She should have given birth to a pair
of hands. Why didn't she just give birth to a
pair of hands?

Why are you here? After all this time…what
sense does it make? Just before I'm getting
out…What do you want from me? Have you
come to fuck me up?

But you… You were wanted… All Aja wanted
was you…

Why did my Aja need you? Was I not enough?
Was I not enough?

Shame and anger drip from his face.

Why are you silent? Say something. Please, say
something…

*His pain gathers even more momentum. His
anger turns on him.*

Here…here…

He wipes his makeup off with his sleeve.

This is who I am. I pushed your mother, okay?

*Wipes off as much of his makeup as he possibly
can. Reveals his full, natural face for the first
time.*

This is your father. This is who I am. Is this what
you want? Hah? You happy now?

I have nothing to offer you…

…except this letter…

He pulls a piece of paper out of his pocket. This is the only real, physical object on stage.

This one letter, I have kept it with me, pasted it onto my cell wall, and stared at it over the years. The same letter that my Olga left me, the one that said, "Dear Felix." The one where I signed my Olga's name at the end.

It's all I have for you. I...I don't have a pen, but...if you want...you could just scratch out her name...and put yours instead.

Tomorrow, I leave this place. But tonight, if you wish, you could complete this letter. In it, you could write:

"Dear Felix, I want nothing to do with you. Ever. Yours, Emma."

Or,

"Dear Felix, I don't know if you can ever be a father to me, but if you would like to meet me sometime, we can sit on a park bench and get to know each other. Yours, Emma."

He looks at her with so much tenderness that it makes him want to hold her face in his hands. He holds the letter against his heart.

"But no matter. Life is good. Life is al-jabr, Flix. All life is al-jabr."

It means, "Reunion of the Broken Parts."

He slowly offers her the letter. All we see is a humbled man, seated in a chair, who has realized, for the first time, that he needs to be there for someone else.

THE END

PLAYWRIGHT'S NOTE AND ACKNOWLEDGEMENTS

My grand-aunt used to paint portraits of clowns. As a child, I was fascinated by one in particular. Just a face: white make-up, red lips. I don't think he had a red nose, but I could be wrong. The eyes were what got me. He looked haunted, as if he were being pursued by someone, or something. "The eyes are the hardest to paint," my grand-aunt would say. That didn't surprise me. Whenever I was alone in that room, I'd stare into his eyes in order to figure out what had happened to him. *What's behind you?* I wanted to know.

I asked myself the same question when it came to some people in my family.

They were great storytellers, and they lived with tremendous chutzpah, but I always got the sense that there was something *not* funny that enabled them to be funny, or carry a joke too far, or be tremendously kind one minute and then turn on a dime the next. The humour came with sadness, some of which was mine. This melancholy came from the idea of impermanence, the realization at a very early age that things did not and could not last. I would look at my grandparents, grand-aunt and -uncles, and want to remain in that moment, partake of their performance and largesse. I wish they were alive today to see *Buffoon*. Felix the clown is an ode to them. In a way, he is them. So now I'm introducing them to you.

Special thanks to Pam Winter and the Gary Godard Agency, the Canada Council for the Arts, Tarragon Theatre, the Arts Club Theatre Company, and the Vancouver Asian Canadian Theatre.

A final note: the aphorism "The two most important days in your life…" is considered Twain apocrypha. It's a common misattribution, so I didn't hold it against whomever Felix heard it from.

Author photograph: Boman Irani

ANOSH IRANI has published four critically acclaimed novels: *The Cripple and His Talismans* (2004), a national bestseller; *The Song of Kahunsha* (2006), which was an international bestseller and a finalist for Canada Reads and the Ethel Wilson Fiction Prize; *Dahanu Road* (2010), which was long-listed for the Man Asian Literary Prize; and *The Parcel* (2016), which was a finalist for the Governor General's Literary Award for Fiction and the Writers' Trust Fiction Prize. His play *Bombay Black* (2006) won the Dora Mavor Moore Award for Outstanding New Play, and his anthology *The Bombay Plays: The Matka King & Bombay Black* (2007) and his play *The Men in White* (2018) were both finalists for the Governor General's Literary Award for Drama. His collection of stories, *Translated from the Gibberish: Seven Stories and One Half Truth*, was published by Knopf in 2019. *Buffoon*, his latest work of drama, was critically acclaimed and won the 2020 Dora Mavor Moore Award for Outstanding New Play. He lives in Vancouver.